QUEENS
OF THE
JUNGLE

**MEET THE FEMALE ANIMALS
WHO RULE THE ANIMAL
KINGDOM!**

NEON  SQUID

CONTENTS

TIME FOR THE QUEENS

Male lions are often referred to as the "Kings of the Jungle" because they are thought to be the strongest, bravest, and fiercest animals in the world. This is a myth. In fact, it's the lionesses that are out hunting together and taking down large animals to feed their entire pride, including the males! Male animals have historically received more attention than females. One major reason for this was that, until relatively recently, the male scientists of our species were the ones getting the most attention. Now that women scientists are starting to get the recognition they deserve, we are finding out more about female animals than ever before.

In this book, I am going to introduce you to the "Queens of the Jungle." These amazing female animals can be found in different habitats all over the world and represent many different species. You will learn about the importance of grandmothers in orca whale societies, the ravenous appetite of black widow spiders, and the beautiful adornments of the female blanket octopus. From building incredible structures to reproducing without the help of males, the females highlighted in this book all have features that make them the wonder women of the animal kingdom.

My name is Carly, and as a female scientist, I am interested in learning all about females across the animal kingdom. I am an animal physiologist, which means I study how animals' bodies have evolved to work with their environment. I am also a biology professor, and I'm dedicated to making sure that the beautiful diversity of the animal kingdom is appreciated by everyone. This book is a collection of my favorite female animals—I hope you like it!

Dr. Carly Anne York

LEADER OF THE PACK

Animals that live in groups, called social species, almost always have a leader. The leader is often responsible for finding resources, like food and water, and keeping things peaceful. People often presume that males make the best leaders—but hold on a second! Let's meet some animals where the females pull the strings.

Don't take me on

Female ring-tailed lemurs are the bosses of the troop. They are the same size as males, and will consistently win fights against any males that challenge their authority. Don't mess with them!

Need a babysitter?

Dwarf mongooses are what are known as cooperative breeders. This means that only one female is allowed to reproduce and everyone in the group helps to raise her offspring.

Horsing around

A herd of wild horses consists of a male, a group of females, and their offspring. The ruler of the herd is usually an older female. Even if she is smaller than the stallion, the herd follows her lead.

Clash of the titans

Typically, males of the animal kingdom fight each other, but when it comes to topi antelope, it's the females that fight for dominance. They even clash over who gets the best mate, which is unusual among female animals.

Elephants express excitement and joy by flapping their ears.

ELEPHANT FEET ARE HIGHLY SENSITIVE AND CAN DETECT THE RUMBLINGS OF OTHER ELEPHANTS THAT ARE MILES AWAY.

MEET THE MATRIARCH

African elephant ♦ Mammal

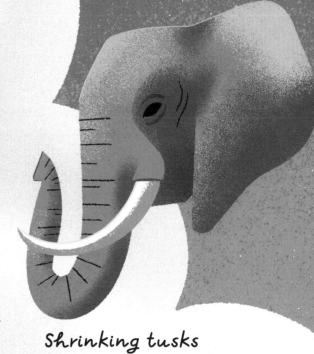

It's all about girl power when it comes to African elephant families, which consist of a matriarch mother, her sisters, daughters, and their babies. The matriarch is often the oldest and largest female in the group, and the family looks to her for direction. The matriarch passes on her knowledge of where to find food, water, and safety to younger members of the family. Wild elephants can live up to the age of 70, so by the time they become a matriarch they have gained many years of wisdom. It just shows, you should always listen to your elders!

Shrinking tusks

Female African elephants have tusks, just like the males. Because elephants with large tusks are targets for poachers, the tusks of both males and females have become smaller than they were a few decades ago. Tuskless elephants are also becoming more common.

Your turn!

Female elephants will teach younger members of the family how to be a good mother by allowing them to babysit, a type of behavior called allomothering.

Killer jaws

Tiny muscles in the head of the trap-jaw ant pull the jaws open and lock them into place with a latch. When the trigger muscle releases the latch, the jaws snap together!

Sensory hairs inside the jaws trigger the jaws to snap shut when prey is detected.

SCIENTISTS MEASURED THE SPEED OF THE SNAPPING JAWS USING HIGH-SPEED VIDEO.

JAW JUMPERS

Trap-jaw ant ♦ Insect

Which creature do you think has the fastest bite in the animal kingdom? A crocodile perhaps? Or a shark? Wrong—the trap-jaw ant is one of the fastest of them all! Only the females of this tropical species have impressive jaws for capturing prey. They can snap their jaws shut 2,300 times faster than the blink of an eye!

Small ant syndrome

Females are the queens and the workers of the trap-jaw ant society. The males, which are called drones, look very different, with wings and a smaller body.

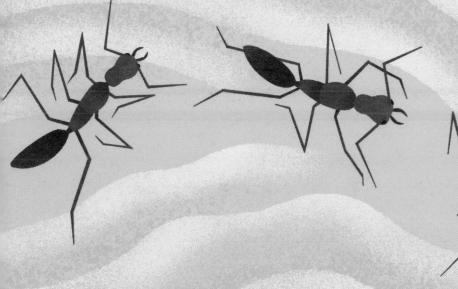

Popcorning

The females snap their jaws so quickly that the force enables them to launch themselves straight into the air! Scientists call this the "popcorn effect." The ants use this tactic to escape from predators. So there's no need to be alarmed if you see somersaulting ants...

SHARING'S CARING

Bonobo ◆ Primate

Bonobos are close relatives of chimpanzees, however there are some big differences between these two primate species. In bonobo societies, the females guide the way! The highest-ranking individuals in the troop are always the older females, while the lower ranks are sex-balanced. The bonobo matriarch will command the troop and have first access to food, which she will generously share with everyone else. This is quite the contrast to chimpanzee societies, where every adult male is dominant over every female. Which society would you prefer to live in?

Home sweet home
Bonobos are only found in the Democratic Republic of Congo, a country in Africa.

BONOBO SOCIETIES CAN CONTAIN MORE THAN 100 INDIVIDUALS.

You scratch my back
Bonobos spend a lot of time grooming and socializing. This is an important way for members of the troop to bond with each other. Who doesn't like a back scratch!

Bonobo

Chimpanzee

A peaceful society
Chimpanzee males will regularly attack and kill both adults and babies from their own and nearby troops. Bonobos, on the other hand, solve issues peacefully and rarely escalate to serious violence.

LISTEN TO YOUR GRANDMOTHER

Orca ♦ Cetacean

Orcas don't think that getting old is a bad thing, and not just because they don't get wrinkles. The most important members of the pod are the grandmothers! They are the most knowledgeable hunters and lead the pod on hunting trips. From the age of 10, a female will give birth roughly every six years until she's about 40. While the males usually only live into their 30s, female orcas can live to be 80 years old! Only a few animal species have females that live for many years after they stop having babies (humans are another one).

Killer whale song

Orcas, also known as killer whales, communicate underwater by making three types of incredibly loud sounds: clicks, whistles, and pulsed calls. These calls can be heard by other orcas from miles away.

Sharing food

The younger orcas follow the grandmother and she teaches them how to find the best hunting spots. She shares up to 90 percent of the food she catches with her family. Nice one, Grandma!

ORCAS ARE THE LARGEST MEMBERS OF THE DOLPHIN FAMILY.

FEEDING FRENZY

Spotted hyena ♦ Mammal

There are many powerful females in the animal kingdom, but arguably none is more formidable than a spotted hyena. Spotted hyenas have a female-dominated hierarchy, meaning the girls are in charge. In fact, no adult male will ever be dominant over a female—a little sister will even call the shots over her big brother! These ladies are also bigger and more aggressive than the boys. They probably evolved to be better fighters as a way of protecting their offspring during violent hyena feeding frenzies. Hyenas aren't known for their table manners...

Ladies first

Higher-ranking females and their offspring have first dibs during feeding time. The males don't get to eat until all of the females have all had their share of the juicest meat. Unlucky lads!

DESPITE THEIR APPEARANCE, HYENAS AREN'T DOGS. THEY'RE ACTUALLY MORE CLOSELY RELATED TO CATS!

Best mom in the world

Hyenas are caring mothers who nurse their cubs for around 14 months. Once the cubs start eating solids, the mothers make sure they have access to food even during a feeding frenzy.

17

Carnivores

Carnivores, like the fossa (a mammal from Madagascar), rely on hunting and killing other animals for food. Fossas will mostly hunt lemurs, but they'll never say no to a fish, bird, mouse, frog, or even wild pig.

DINNER IS SERVED

Across the animal kingdom it is up to females to search high and low to provide meals for themselves and their babies. Depending on the species, they do this in different ways—from hunting other animals and eating plants to scavenging meals left behind by others.

Herbivores

Some of the largest animals in the world, including our distant cousin, the gorilla, rely solely on plants for their incredible strength. All of a gorilla's nutritional needs are met without ever eating meat. Animals that only eat plants are called herbivores.

Upside down

Flamingos are filter feeders. These birds feed with their heads upside down, using their large beaks to collect food from the water. They get their pink color from the shrimp and algae they eat!

Scavengers

Scavengers are incredibly important for the health of an ecosystem because they help to clean up after animals have died. Vultures consume huge amounts of rotting flesh every day!

Omnivores

A wild boar is an example of an omnivore, an animal that eats plants and meat. They're the opposite of fussy eaters! Wild boars happily snuffle up fallen fruit, nuts, plants, and occasionally small mammals and eggs.

Gulp!

Some animals, like snakes, don't have proper teeth for chewing their food. Instead, they use a technique called bulk feeding that allows them to eat their prey by swallowing it whole!

EMPEROR PENGUINS CAN REACH DEPTHS OF MORE THAN 1,650 FT (500 M).

Hold your breath!

Emperor penguins can dive deeper than any other bird. Typically, they dive for around 5 minutes at a time, but they can hold their breath for up to 22 minutes!

Don't drop the egg!

After the female passes the egg to the male, he keeps it off the frozen ground by holding it on his feet.

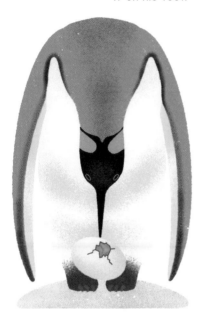

Seconds, anyone?

The mother emperor penguin catches fish and partially digests it. When she reaches her chick, she coughs the mixture back up and the chick eats it directly from her bill!

DEEP DIVERS

Emperor penguin ♦ Bird

Emperor penguins breed during the Antarctic winter. For the female, it's the start of an epic adventure. After she lays her egg, she carefully passes it to the male. She must really trust him, because she spends the next two months traveling to the ocean and fishing! She's not on a girls' retreat, though, but busy finding food to bring back for her newborn. The female emperor penguin returns with a belly full of fish around the time the egg hatches—perfect timing!

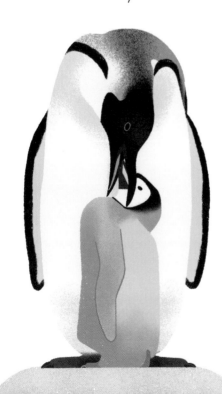

TEACHING THE WAY

Polar bear ◆ Mammal

Hitching a ride

When the cubs are born they haven't yet developed the fur and fat insulation that will keep them warm. Mothers often carry cubs on their back through deep snow to keep them protected from the cold.

She may look cuddly, but there's no fiercer hunter in the harsh, snowy conditions of the Arctic than a female polar bear. There's a good reason she's such a fearsome predator— she has cubs to look after and, since the males don't stick around to look after their young, it's down to her to raise them alone. Polar bears love eating seals, but they also won't turn their noses up at a whale carcass or bird eggs. The cubs watch their mother catch food for their first year and pay close attention, learning the crucial hunting skills they'll need for when it's time for them to venture out alone.

Cosy den

Polar bear cubs are born in dens dug into the snow. These dens provide a safe environment for the fragile newborn cubs. After going months without any food, the mother pokes a hole in the snow. It's time to emerge!

TREASURE HUNTING
IN THE SNOW

Reindeer ◆ Mammal

Female reindeer have a special feature that is usually only found on male deer—antlers! One reason why female reindeer evolved to grow antlers is because of their cold tundra habitat. In these harsh environments, with no trees and very little vegetation, food is often frozen under layers of snow. That's where the antlers come in. Females with larger antlers have a better chance of finding something to eat because they can use them to dig food out of the frozen ground. What a lifesaver!

REINDEER SHED THEIR ANTLERS AND GROW NEW ONES EVERY YEAR.

Heavy load

Female antlers are often smaller than male antlers. Of all the deer species alive today, reindeer have the largest and heaviest antlers compared to their body size.

Keeping safe

A reindeer's antlers are also good weapons for self-defense. Males lose their antlers in the fall, but females keep their antlers until their calves are born in the late spring.

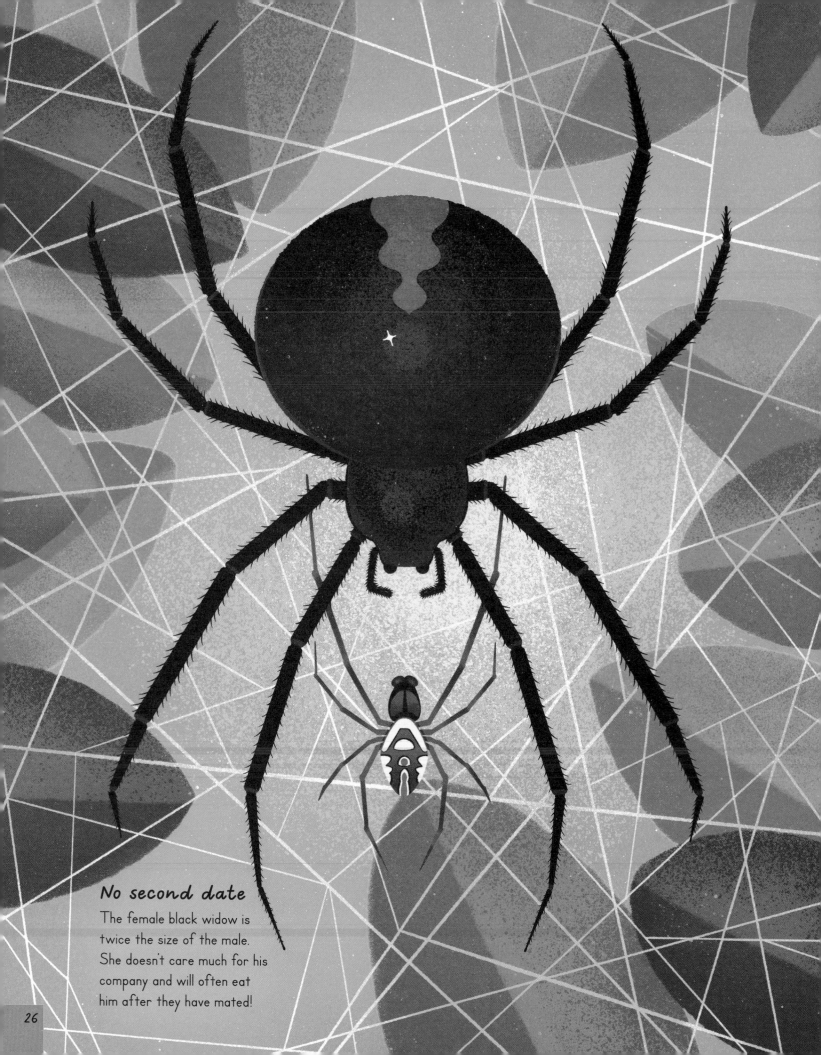

No second date

The female black widow is twice the size of the male. She doesn't care much for his company and will often eat him after they have mated!

BEWARE THE WIDOW!

Black widow ♦ Arachnid

When it comes to black widow spiders, it's the females you need to be wary of. She quietly waits in her web for unsuspecting insects to come her way. When she feels something has got stuck in her web, she charges toward the intruder and bites. She sinks her fangs into her prey, but she doesn't only injure it—she also injects deadly neurotoxins! These paralyze her prey and turn their insides into goo. She then wraps up her prey in a cocoon. This fearsome spider isn't too fussy about what she eats—she's even partial to males of her own species. Watch out, boys!

Spidey senses
The black widow has eight eyes but relies on the hair on her legs to feel vibrations in the web—the tell-tale sign of trapped prey.

Packed lunch
The cocoon preserves the prey for later if the spider has recently eaten. When she is hungry she will suck up the insides of her prey while it is still trapped in the cocoon.

FIGHT FOR YOUR PRIDE

Lion ✦ Big cat

A male lion's large size and flowy mane may look impressive, but behind every king of the jungle is a team of queens. After all, it's the lionesses who do all of the hard work! The lionesses catch and kill most of the prey for a pride of lions, working as elite commando units in the darkness of night. They're also responsible for defending their territory from other lions, including other females looking for territories of their own. While these fierce ladies know how to defend themselves, they show a softer side when raising the cubs. They will care for each other's cubs as well as their own!

Looking for trouble

Almost all the members of a lion pride are related females. The males, on the other hand, go from pride to pride, spending most of their time fighting each other.

Teamwork makes the dream work

Lionesses are smaller and more agile than the males. They often go out in small groups and work as a team to stalk and kill large prey, such as buffaloes.

Patience is a virtue

After the lionesses make a kill, the males swoop in and dine first. Once they're done, the lionesses and the cubs get the leftovers. They will ferociously defend their kill against any other predators, like hyenas, that try to muscle in on the feast.

PUTTING ON A SHOW

When it comes to choosing a mate, female animals have all the power. As a result, male animals have developed different ways to impress the ladies—from wild colors to silly dances! When males and females of the same species look different it is called sexual dimorphism.

Flashing flaps

Female fan-throated lizards love to see a brightly colored patch of skin under a male's throat. To really knock her socks off, the male flashes his throat flap and bobs his heads.

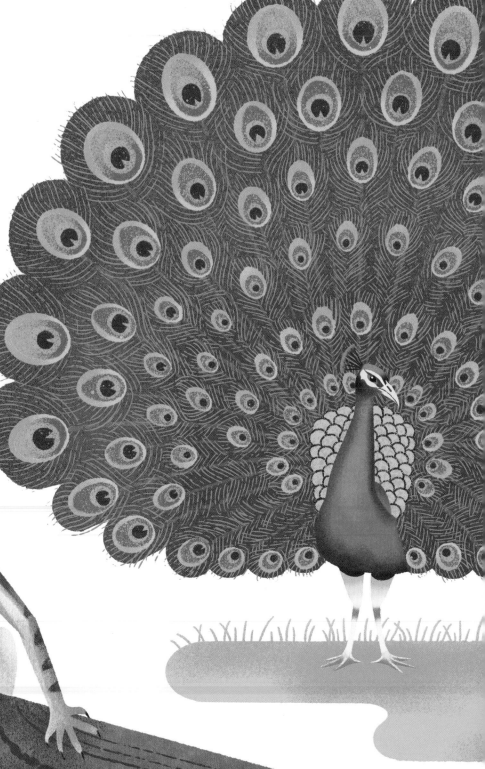

Not so private parts

Female mandrills are attracted to bright colors on the male in two places—their faces and, believe it or not, their butts!

Rainbow feathers

Female peacocks can't resist a male peacock's large, colorful tail feathers. When he is trying to impress her, the male peacock will open his tail and shake it to catch the light— what a display!

Bust a move

Female peacock spiders are quite picky. Seeing a brightly colored abdomen on the male isn't enough—they also want to see them show off a few moves! The males dance and sing through vibrations to impress the females.

LOOK AT ME NOW

Mediterranean parrotfish ♦ Fish

Nature is full of male animals with bold, vibrant colors. Looking at you, peacocks. Parrotfish, however, flip the script. In this fish species, it is the females that have dazzing colors! Male parrotfish, by contrast, are gray and dull. The parrotfish spend their days nibbling on the coral reefs they call home. Coral is tough to chew, but it is no contest for their powerful beaks. Scientists have discovered that parrotfish have the strongest teeth in the world. Not only that, but they also have extra teeth in their throat that help to break up tough food!

Beginner level

Young Mediterranean parrotfish are neither male nor female. They are quite small, with a gray mottled pattern and a yellowish head.

Pooping sandcastles

When parrotfish poop out the coral they have digested, what comes out the other end is sand! In one year, a single parrotfish can produce 1,000 lb (450 kg) of sand—that's about the same weight as a grand piano!

PARROTFISH HAVE ROUGHLY 1,000 TEETH. THEY WOULD TAKE A WHILE TO BRUSH...

Changing looks

When the parrotfish get their adult colors they develop into either females or males. The females have such vivid colors to attract males.

33

Bird of prey

The northern goshawk can be found throughout Europe, Asia, and North America. This master hunter enjoys eating squirrels, rabbits, and medium-sized birds such as crows.

THE BIGGER THE BETTER

Northern goshawk ✦ Bird

Northern goshawks have a characteristic not often seen in birds or mammals—the females are about 25 percent heavier than males! When there's a noticeable size difference between females and males it's called size dimorphism. But, since the female goshawks are the ones that are larger, they call this a case of reverse size dimorphism. Scientists aren't sure why female goshawks are bigger than males. One idea is that it's so the pair can feed on a wider range of prey, including large and small animals. This makes them a real dream team! The males aren't bad hunters by any stretch, but the females are next-level assassins, capable of taking down animals the same size as them.

On the hunt

During breeding season, the larger female protects the nest while the male is responsible for bringing food back to her and their chicks.

Old favorites

Goshawk pairs can build up to eight different nests in their nesting area. Despite this, they might just choose to the use the same one year after year!

THE LATIN NAME OF THIS SPECIES MEANS "NOBLE HAWK" BECAUSE ONLY THE NOBILITY COULD USE THEM FOR FALCONRY IN THE MIDDLE AGES!

THE NAKED QUEEN

Naked mole-rat ♦ Rodent

The naked mole-rat may not be winning beauty pageants around the world, but she is beautifully adapted to her life underground. She has almost no hair, no external ears, and is virtually blind. But since she lives in tunnels of dirt, she does just fine! Naked mole-rats are eusocial, which means they live in a large group where one female is the queen and gives birth to all the babies, much like in a beehive. The queen usually gives birth to around 12 babies at a time. Everyone else, called the workers, spend their entire lives maintaining and defending the burrow system. This is pretty useful—with 12 babies this mom won't be getting much time to herself!

Underground buffet

Naked mole-rats mostly eat plants and roots they find underground.

Maternal care

During her pregnancy, the queen's spine will get longer to make room for the growing pups. She breeds with a few males in the colony, and all of the other individuals in the group help her raise her offspring.

THE OCTOPUS WITH THE SUPERHERO CAPE

Blanket octopus ◆ *Cephalopod*

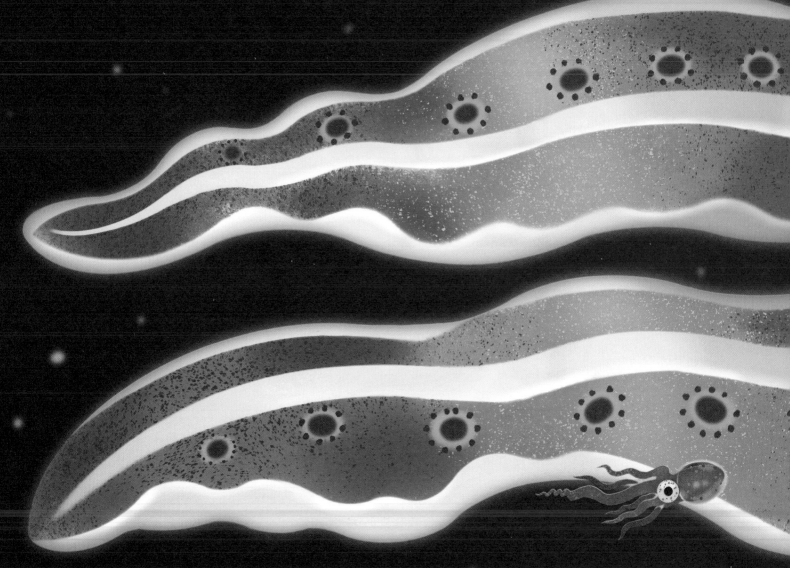

MALES OF THIS SPECIES ARE ONLY ABOUT THE SIZE OF A WALNUT.

Opposites attract

Male blanket octopuses are tiny, don't have a beautiful cape, and can be up to 40,000 times lighter than the female! They're only about 1 in (2.5 cm) long, while the female grows to 80 in (200 cm). This is the most extreme size dimorphism on the planet!

this is definitely true of this funky animal. Named after the flowing iridescent skin that connects four of her arms, the blanket octopus can unfurl this spectacular cape to make herself look bigger when threatened by a predator. She can also swim away quickly using jet propulsion or release ink to confuse any animals that fancy her as a snack. In extreme cases, she can even break off portions of her cape to distract her pursuer while she makes her getaway. It's so much more than a fashion statement!

Neat trick

Blanket octopuses are immune to the stinging tentacles of the venomous Portuguese man o' war (a jellyfish-like animal). Because of this, they will steal tentacles from it to use as weapons to defend themselves or as a stun gun to knock out their prey!

Female

Male

HIDE-AND-SEEK

Orchid mantis ♦ Insect

Female orchid mantises are spectacularly beautiful
and can easily be mistaken for a delicate flower blossom.
These insects evolved to look this way to catch their prey.
Instead of waiting for an insect to approach a flower, they
stand as still as a statue to confuse their prey into thinking
that they *are* the flower. And voila—an easy catch! While
the female is stunning, the male is…slightly different. He is
only half the size of his counterpart and rather drab in
comparison! The males tend to be more nervous and
agitated, especially in the presence of a female. They have
a good reason: if the female is hungry after they mate,
she might just decide to eat him!

FEMALE ORCHID
MANTISES CAN ALSO
CHANGE THEIR
COLOR LIKE A
CHAMELEON!

Happy together

Sociable weaver birds create enormous nests. Up to 500 weaver birds create the nest together, and it is so sturdy that it can house many birds for decades.

AMAZING ARCHITECTS

If you think humans are the only animals who like to live in a nice house, think again! Many animals are skilled in creating the structures that they call home. These constructions keep them safe from wind, rain, and sunshine—just like our houses protect us. They're also places where they can hide from predators and raise their babies.

Tiny termites

Can you believe something as small as termites are responsible for these gigantic mounds? Termites work together to make these tower blocks out of soil, animal poop, and termite saliva—eww!

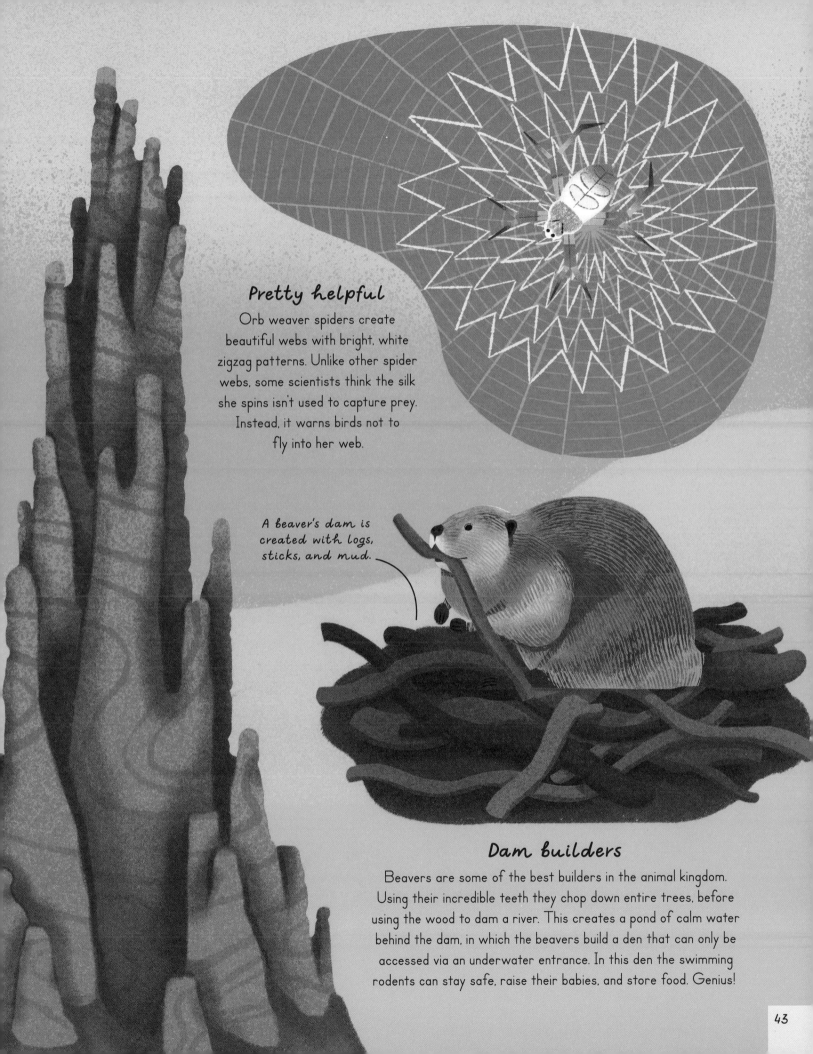

Pretty helpful

Orb weaver spiders create beautiful webs with bright, white zigzag patterns. Unlike other spider webs, some scientists think the silk she spins isn't used to capture prey. Instead, it warns birds not to fly into her web.

A beaver's dam is created with logs, sticks, and mud.

Dam builders

Beavers are some of the best builders in the animal kingdom. Using their incredible teeth they chop down entire trees, before using the wood to dam a river. This creates a pond of calm water behind the dam, in which the beavers build a den that can only be accessed via an underwater entrance. In this den the swimming rodents can stay safe, raise their babies, and store food. Genius!

Treehouse

Once inside, the female molts some of her tail and flight feathers and uses them to line the nest. And what about when she needs the bathroom? She manages to poop out of the opening of the nest!

THE PERFECT HIDING PLACE

Great hornbill ◆ Bird

The female great hornbill builds one of the most remarkable nests in the animal kingdom—and it's all to keep her chicks safe from predators. First, she hides in a hole in a tree and lines it with mud to keep it warm. Then she lays her eggs, before sealing off the entrance to the nest, with her inside! How does she survive, you might wonder? Well, she's completely in the hands (or wings) of her mate. She leaves a small slit in the sealed hole so the male can serve her food. Incubating the eggs is hard work, so she needs him to bring her lots of berries and insects. Once the chicks have hatched and are half grown, the female breaks out of the nest and the chicks reseal the hole. They will stay there until they are ready to face the world.

MALE HORNBILLS CAN CARRY ALMOST 60 PIECES OF FRUIT AT ONCE.

Sticking together

Before mating, the male gains the female's trust through courtship displays. He also brings her lots of snacks! Hornbills only have one mate for each season because of the bond required for this nesting process. Trust is very important for this pair!

SLEEPING IN THE CLOUDS

Orangutan ♦ Primate

Orangutans live in the rainforests of the islands of Borneo and Sumatra in Southeast Asia. It's here that the female orangutan creates some of the sturdiest and most extravagant nests in the animal kingdom. She's a very skilled engineer—there's no way she would stack branches together without a plan. Once she chooses a place on a sturdy branch, the female bends branches toward her and weaves them together to create a platform. On top of that base, she adds small branches and leaves to create a mattress. She can also plait branches above her head to make a roof that keeps the rain out!

Luxury bedding
To make herself and her baby comfortable, the female orangutan creates blankets out of large leafy branches, and makes pillows by clumping leaves together.

ORANGUTANS MAKE A NEW NEST EVERY DAY.

Twisting twigs
Orangutans have learned to break branches off trees by twisting them. Once twisted, it's surprisingly hard to fully snap a branch in half. This means that the nest can hold the weight of a large orangutan and her baby.

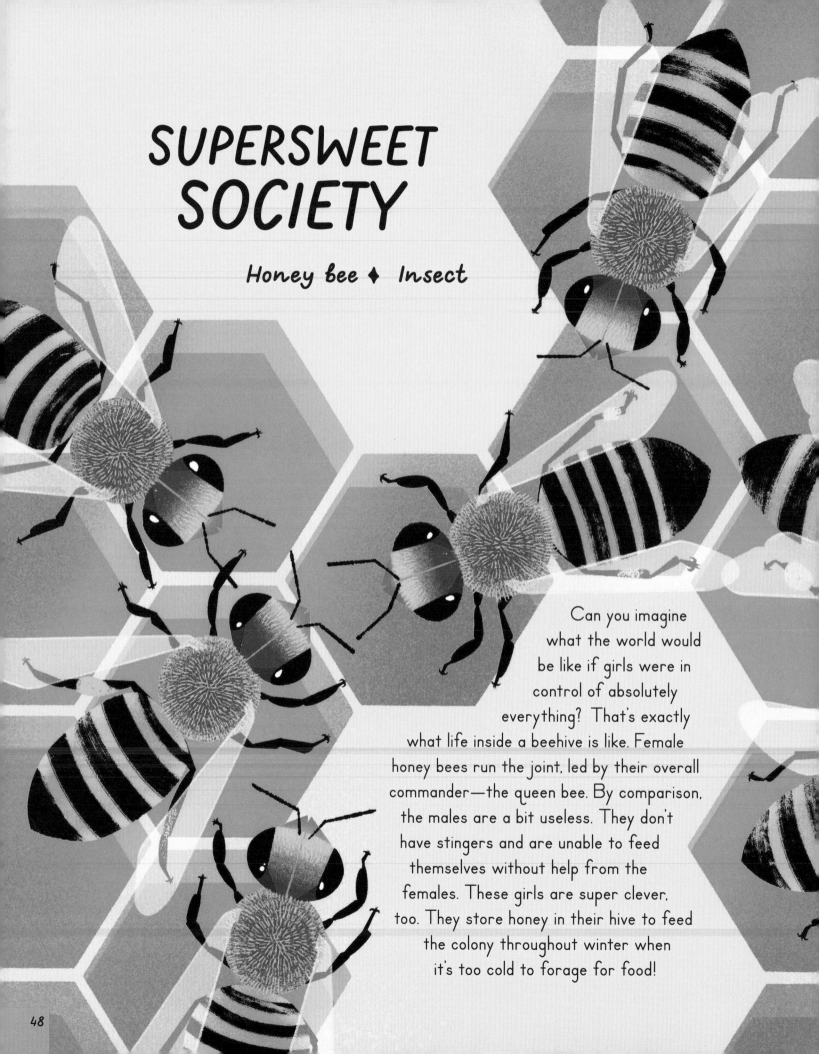

SUPERSWEET SOCIETY

Honey bee ◆ Insect

Can you imagine what the world would be like if girls were in control of absolutely everything? That's exactly what life inside a beehive is like. Female honey bees run the joint, led by their overall commander—the queen bee. By comparison, the males are a bit useless. They don't have stingers and are unable to feed themselves without help from the females. These girls are super clever, too. They store honey in their hive to feed the colony throughout winter when it's too cold to forage for food!

Feeding a hungry crowd

A worker honey bee gathers nectar from different flowers to bring back to the hive. When she returns, she transfers the nectar from her mouth to another worker's mouth. It'll turn into honey in their stomach—yummy!

QUEENS ONLY EAT ROYAL JELLY, A SPECIAL SUBSTANCE PRODUCED BY THE WORKER BEES.

She deserves a crown

The queen is the center of attention (and everything else) in a healthy beehive. She will likely be the only queen in a colony of thousands of bees. The queen is usually the mother of all the bees in the beehive and everyone will fiercely protect her.

SAFE AND SOUND IN THE TREES

Hummingbird ♦ Bird

Fast learners

Hummingbirds begin flapping their wings at two weeks old and can fly less than a month after hatching! Hummingbirds are also one of the only groups of birds that can learn sounds by imitating them.

HUMMINGBIRDS ARE THE ONLY BIRDS THAT CAN FLY BACKWARD.

There are few things in nature as precious as a hummingbird's nest. Female hummingbirds go high up in the trees to build these tiny, delicate structures far away from predators. Picture the softest bed you can: that's what this nest feels like! The moms create soft little cups with flexible sides that can stretch as the baby chicks grow. They use fuzzy plants to make it comfy, and silk from a spider's web to bind everything together and anchor the nest to a tree. Despite being so dainty, these nests provide a safe sanctuary in which the chicks can start their lives.

Mini eggs

Hummingbird eggs are extremely small. They weigh less than a paperclip and are about the size of a jellybean! The nest in this illustration is life-size!

GETTING COZY

Grizzly bear ♦ Mammal

Have you ever been so tired you felt like you could sleep for days? Well, for a grizzly bear that's not so out of the ordinary. Every year, the female grizzly embarks on a mission: to dig a perfect den where she can stay warm while she hibernates through the cold winter months. The den needs to be safe and super cozy, but not just because she wants a luxury pad to snuggle down in—it's also where she will give birth to her cubs! Digging the den is a serious construction job. This industrious bear will spend several days moving up to a ton of dirt!

GRIZZLY BEARS DO NOT EAT, DRINK, POOP, OR PEE DURING HIBERNATION.

The perfect location

Female grizzlies are very picky when it comes to finding the right place to dig their den. Their dream scenario is a den at the base of a tree on a hillside facing north. Why so specific? Well, by facing their den in this direction they ensure that the maximum amount of snow will fall on it, creating layers of insulation. This keeps it snug and warm inside even during the most extreme temperatures.

Food o'clock

Female grizzly bears and their cubs emerge from their den in the late spring. The first thing they'll do is look for a meal. After months without any tasty snacks, it's no wonder they're hungry!

EGG-CELLENT MOTHERS

Survival of the fittest

Fish and amphibians lay jellylike eggs that need to stay moist so that they don't dry out. This means that the animals need to stay in or near a body of water at all times. Usually, these species will lay hundreds of eggs because only a few survive.

Making moves

Reptiles and birds (and even a few mammals) lay amniotic eggs. These eggs contain an internal sac that prevents water from escaping, allowing these species to move away from bodies of water. This was a major step in evolution because it meant animals could venture into new habitats, like deserts and mountains.

Female animals are responsible for bringing the next generation of their species into the world, and more than 99 percent of animals do this with eggs. Eggs provide both nutrients and protection to the unhatched baby (also known as an embryo). Female animals lay different types of eggs depending on their species. Let's have a look at a few!

MANY BABY ANIMALS HAVE A SPECIAL EGG TOOTH TO HELP THEM BREAK OUT OF THE SHELL.

Ultimate protection

Some snakes give birth to live young, but the majority of snakes lay soft, leathery eggs. In some cases, the female coils around the nest to keep her eggs safe.

The award goes to...

Female ostriches lay the largest eggs of any living bird species. A single egg can weigh up to a whopping 5 lb (2.2 kg).

The female giant Pacific octopus spends the next few months waving her arms gently over the eggs so they get plenty of oxygen. She also defends her underwater lair from any potential predators, such as hungry fish looking for an easy snack.

THE ULTIMATE SACRIFICE

Giant Pacific octopus ◆ Cephalopod

The giant Pacific octopus is one of the most generous and loving mothers in the animal kingdom. After mating, she carries fertilized eggs inside her for about five months. She waits until the winter, when the water is the perfect temperature for her to release them. Then she produces a staggering 50,000 eggs, which float free until she gathers them and stitches them into hanging braids. She delicately hangs the eggs in an underwater cave. And then the hard work begins...

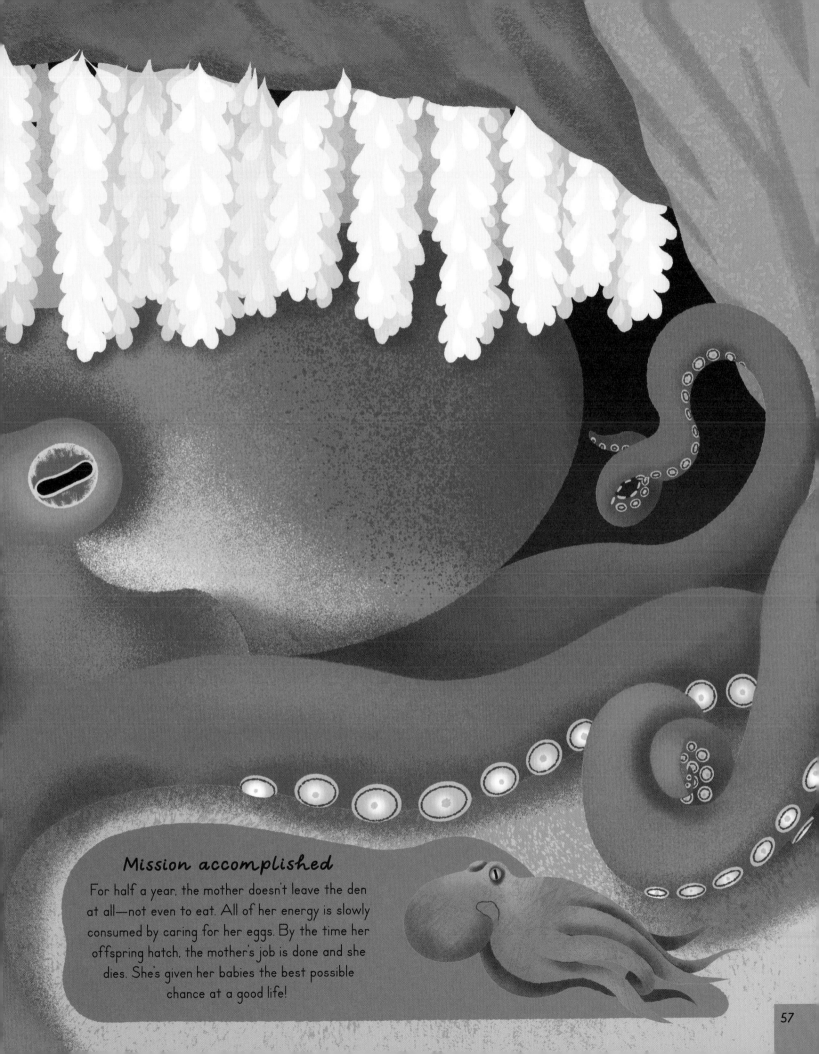

Mission accomplished

For half a year, the mother doesn't leave the den at all—not even to eat. All of her energy is slowly consumed by caring for her eggs. By the time her offspring hatch, the mother's job is done and she dies. She's given her babies the best possible chance at a good life!

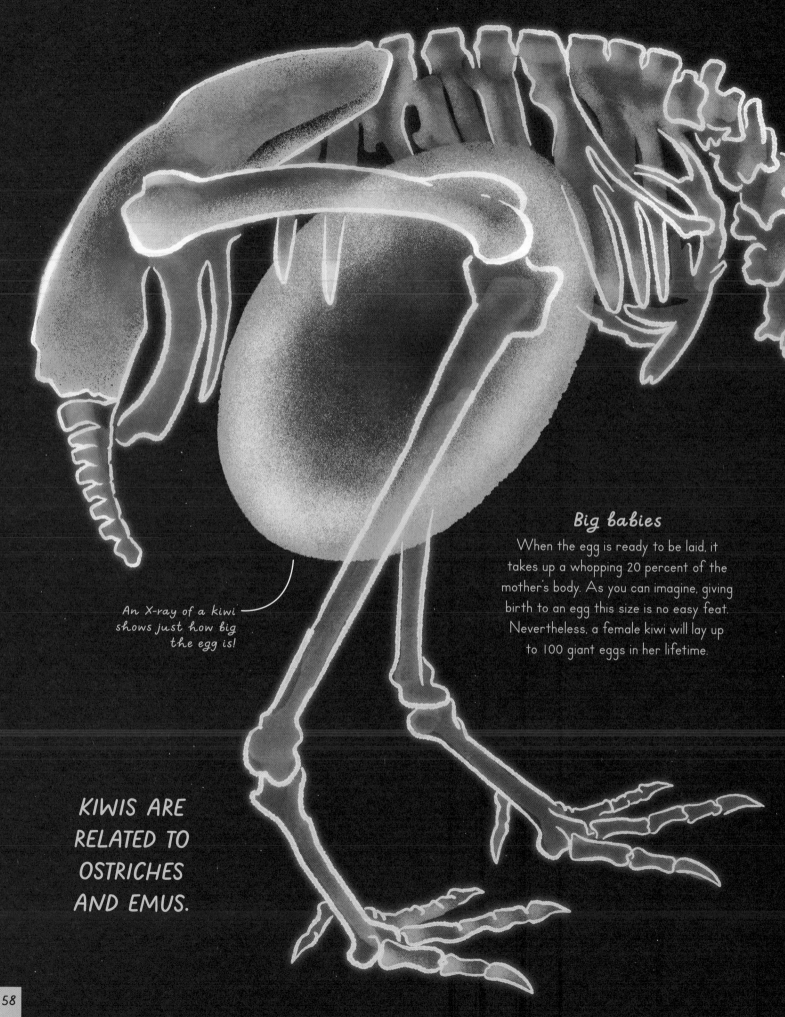

An X-ray of a kiwi shows just how big the egg is!

Big babies

When the egg is ready to be laid, it takes up a whopping 20 percent of the mother's body. As you can imagine, giving birth to an egg this size is no easy feat. Nevertheless, a female kiwi will lay up to 100 giant eggs in her lifetime.

KIWIS ARE RELATED TO OSTRICHES AND EMUS.

THE KIWI AND THE GIANT EGG

Kiwi ♦ Bird

You may have heard of the kiwi, a bird native to New Zealand. Kiwis aren't particularly big, but they lay incredibly large eggs! In fact, kiwi eggs are about six times bigger than other birds of the same size. The female kiwi lays an egg that can weigh up to a quarter of her body weight. Proportionally, this is by far the largest egg of any bird in the world. It's like a human giving birth to a four-year-old child. Ouch!

Fake it 'til you make it

Kiwis are flightless birds but they are so "unbird-like" that many scientists call them honorary mammals. Kiwi feathers have even evolved into soft, fur-like fibres to suit their life on the ground. These birds are nocturnal (active at night) and have a fantastic sense of smell so they can find earthworms in the dark.

THE MYSTERY OF THE COLORFUL EGGS

Growing up

Although baby stink bugs (nymphs) are similar in shape to the adults, they are much smaller and often change color as they mature.

Eggs hatch and develop into adults in as little as 40 days.

Clever chemistry

A chemical compound called melanin is used to produce dark colors in insects. However, the stink bug eggs are not colored using this compound. Do they have a magic paintbrush hidden somewhere?

STINK BUGS GOT THEIR NAME FOR A REASON— THEY SMELL LIKE ROTTING VEGETABLES!

Stink bug ♦ Insect

Female stink bugs have a special trick for keeping their offspring safe from predators and the glaring sun—they can change the color of their eggs! They lay eggs in a range of different colors, from pale yellow to black, to suit the conditions of where they are laid. Eggs laid on the tops of leaves tend to be darker, which protects them from the sun. However, eggs laid on the underside of leaves don't need protection from the sun, so the stink bug mom makes them a lighter color. These clever critters are currently the only animals known to control the color of their eggs by choice. How they do it is a mystery!

A platypus can detect food underwater using its sensitive bill. It eats worms, shellfish, and insects.

Platypus ♦ Monotreme

It's common for reptiles and birds to lay eggs, but egg-laying mammals are incredibly rare. Enter the platypus! This bizarre animal from Australia looks like it has been cobbled together from different animals. It has fur like an otter, a beak and feet like a duck, and a tail like a beaver! The female platypus hides away in an underground burrow to lay her eggs, before keeping them warm by placing them on her body. The babies are born completely helpless, and the mother nurses them with milk until they can swim on their own.

A BABY PLATYPUS IS ONLY ABOUT THE SIZE OF A PENNY WHEN IT EMERGES FROM ITS EGG.

DON'T PLAY BY THE RULES

Safe and sound

The mother digs a nesting burrow along the bank of a river or stream and creates a nest using wet leaves. When she leaves the burrow, she plugs the exit with soil to protect her babies.

BUILDING THE PERFECT HOUSE

Argonaut ♦ Cephalopod

The argonaut is a relative of the octopus, but instead of spending her days crawling around the ocean floor like her distant cousin, she floats near the surface. This means that while a female octopus can hide her eggs in nooks and crannies, the female argonaut needs to be more creative. She can't find a home for her eggs, so she builds one from scratch! After she mates, she creates her shell by producing a substance called calcite from her arms. Only female argonauts have this special ability.

A tight squeeze

After the mother creates a shell and lays her eggs inside, she squeezes her body into it.

Coming out of my shell

A female argonaut can lay more than 40,000 eggs inside her shell. The baby argonauts do not grow shells while they are in the eggs, but they can produce a shell within hours of hatching.

The female argonaut grips on to her shell using her arms. She can release it at any time.

THE SHELL TRAPS AIR, WHICH HELPS THE FEMALE ARGONAUT TO FLOAT.

Mammals

Genes are contained in threadlike structures called chromosomes. In some animals chromosomes determine whether an animal is male or female. Mammals, like wolves, have XX chromosomes if they are female and XY chromosomes if they are male. Only the male has a Y chromosome, which means he contributes the genes that determine the sex of the cubs.

NICE GENES

Why do males and females even exist? The answer lies in something called genes. Genes are special instructions that dictate what an animal looks like and how healthy it will be. When animals choose a mate, they are looking for a partner that will pass on the healthiest genes to their babies. In most species, both the female and the male will contribute their genes, in the form of egg and sperm, to produce the next generation of offspring. But that's not always the case...

Ducks

Birds, like ducks, also have their sex determined through chromosomes. Their chromosomes are ZW for females and ZZ for males. This means that the female is the one that contributes the genes that determine the sex of the ducklings.

Tortoises

The temperature of a tortoise's nest determines whether the offspring will be male or female, not their chromosomes. If the temperature is warm the eggs develop into females, but if the nest is cool the eggs turn into males.

Ants

The sex of an ant is determined by whether or not its egg was fertilized by a male. Female ants come from fertilized eggs, whereas male ants develop from unfertilized eggs. Fertilized eggs contain chromosomes from both parents, which means that female ants have twice the number of chromosomes as male ants!

A STING IN THE TAIL

Stuff him!

Female paper wasps are not fond of sharing their food. They will stuff the males headfirst into empty holes in the nest to stop them having their fill!

Paper wasp ◆ Insect

Life is tough if you're a paper wasp. The chances are that you won't survive through the cold winter. Unless you're a queen wasp, that is... These royal insects survive the freezing temperatures by nesting in warm crevices, such as in the bark of trees. With the warmth of spring, the queens crawl out of their snuggly dens and join other queens to start a new nest. While they work together at first, eventually one queen comes to dominate all of the others. She then makes them serve as workers for her new colony! The dominant queen focuses on laying eggs, while the workers build the nest and feed the young (larvae). Because the stinger on a wasp developed from the ovipositor, the structure used for laying eggs, only female wasps can sting!

Male

Female

Boys and girls

Male and female paper wasps look similar, but their facial markings distinguish them from each other. Females have more black markings on their face, while males are more yellow.

Paper home

Paper wasps get their name from the way they make their nests. First they chew wood into a pulp. Then they mold this papery substance into the shape of an umbrella.

CLOWNING AROUND

Clownfish ◆ Fish

Meet the family

A group of clownfish includes one dominant female and one dominant male, who are a breeding pair, and several youngsters, who will develop into males as they grow.

Underwater pals

Clownfish have a special mucus that protects them from stinging sea anemones, so they hide in their tentacles to stay safe from predators. In return, the clownfish clean parasites off the anemones.

Whether an animal is male or female is not always a simple question. When it comes to clownfish, the answer can change over their lifetime! Clownfish live in groups that are led by a dominant female. She is no pushover and will display aggressive behavior to keep her position as top fish. There's something particularly interesting about this female: she was once a male! Every time a clownfish group loses its dominant female, the next male in the hierarchy changes into a female and takes over her role.

Congratulations on your promotion

When the dominant female dies, the clownfish chain of command kicks in. The dominant male becomes the next dominant female. The next male in the hierarchy will take the position of dominant male.

THE TEMPERATURE IN THE ROOM

Crocodile ◆ Reptile

With their sharp teeth and scaly skin, crocodiles strike fear into many animals. But did you know that female crocodiles are very attentive mothers? They carefully build a nest for their precious eggs. Typically, the nest is either a hole in the ground or it is made of sticks. These nests are important because, aside from protecting the eggs, they also keep them at a steady temperature. The right temperature is key for the development of many species, but for crocodiles, it is especially important. The temperature of the eggs while they are incubating in the nest determines whether the hatchlings will be male or female!

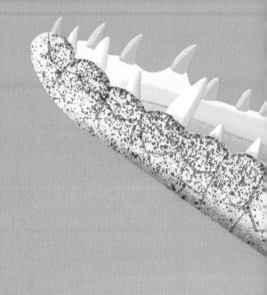

Female babies

Male babies

Female babies

Girls are cool

When the eggs are kept at lower temperatures, the hatchlings will be female. Once the temperature has reached around 86°F (30°C), the eggs switch to males. However, if the eggs become a few degrees warmer, they switch back to being females!

Don't bite!

When the babies are ready to hatch, they chirp for help from their mother. She picks up each egg and rolls it gently in her mouth until it hatches. Then she carries the new hatchling to the water!

FEMALE CROCODILES CARE FOR THEIR BABIES FOR SEVERAL MONTHS AFTER THEY HATCH.

SECRETS OF THE ROCK POOL

Ribbed Mediterranean limpet

◆ Snail

Somewhere to shell-ter

Once a female, the limpet can produce up to 1,000 eggs. After they've been fertilized by a male, she will protect them in her shell before releasing them as free-swimming larvae.

Upside-down

Limpets have a large foot for crawling around, but they spend most of their life anchored in one place. They are filter feeders, and feast on algae and phytoplankton that drift by.

If you peer into a rock pool there's a good chance you'll see a sea snail anchored to a rock. If you thought these animals were simple, think again! The ribbed Mediterranean limpet is a sex-changing species. These sea snails begin their lives as males and become females once they have reached a certain size. Scientists believe that the reason they become females when they are bigger is so they can produce more eggs. The change from male to female is usually initiated when the limpets bump up against each other.

Mini me
Some species of chameleons, like Jackson's chameleon, live in the mountains where it is too cold to lay eggs. Instead, they give live birth to between 8 and 30 little chameleons!

LIVE BIRTH

Instead of laying an egg, many female animals give birth to live babies—just like humans! This reproductive strategy provides several benefits for the female. For example, she doesn't need to guard a nest and can move about while her unborn offspring develops inside her.

Big baby
Newborn blue whales are the biggest babies in the animal kingdom—when they are born they're about the size of a small car! A female blue whale is pregnant for around a year, and she can give birth every two to three years.

Something fishy going on

Most fish lay eggs, but some species, such as the guppy, give live birth to baby fish. The female guppy carries the offspring inside her for about a month before giving birth.

Long drop

Female giraffes are pregnant for a very long time—up to 15 months. Giraffes give birth standing up, which means there is about a 6 ft (1.8 m) drop to the ground when the baby is born! This doesn't hurt the baby giraffe, in fact the impact helps stimulate them to take their first breath.

JOEYS POOP AND PEE IN THE POUCH SO THE MOTHER NEEDS TO CLEAN IT REGULARLY.

Follow the trail

A joey is born hairless and blind after only a month of developing in the womb. After it has been born, the joey follows a trail of saliva the mother has left for it to crawl its way up her body to her pouch. Not bad for a newborn!

MEET THE SUPERMOM

Kangaroo ◆ Marsupial

Female kangaroos are the queens of multitasking—they can raise up to three baby kangaroos of different ages at the same time! These Australian animals are a type of mammal called a marsupial. This means they give birth to very small, undeveloped babies, called joeys, that spend several months growing inside a special pouch on the female. Because of her clever parenting strategy, a female kangaroo can have one joey in her womb, one joey in her pouch, and another older joey bouncing alongside her!

A joey's life

A joey will spend about half a year growing inside of its mother's pouch. During this time, it will grow from the size of a gummy bear until it is large enough to hop around on its own.

A BABY'S RATTLE

Rattlesnake ◆ Reptile

While many species of snakes lay leathery eggs, female rattlesnakes, found in North and South America, give birth to live young. This snake is one of only a few reptiles that care for their newborn offspring. She protects her brood until they shed their skin for the first time, usually after a week. After this, the young leave their mom and must look after themselves. Rattlesnakes get their name from the rattle on the end of their tail. A segment is added to the rattle each time the snake sheds its skin, so the babies can't rattle until they shed for a second time. If surprised or alarmed, they will shake this rattle to warn others to stay away!

Sss-special delivery

A female rattlesnake can give birth to up to 20 baby snakes at a time.

Deadly babies

The newborn snakes look like miniature adults, and they pack a punch! Just like the adults, baby rattlesnakes have needle-sharp fangs and deadly venom. You don't want to mess with these babies!

MOTHER OF ALL SHARKS

Great white sharks locate their prey using their strong sense of smell.

Great white shark ♦ Fish

Great white sharks are apex predators, feared throughout the ocean. They also have an unusual way of giving birth, although no one has ever got close enough to witness it first hand! First the sharks grow their young, called pups, in eggs inside them. But then, instead of laying these eggs like many other shark species, the eggs hatch while they are still inside the mother! This process is called ovoviviparity. The females then give birth to several pups at a time, each of which is about 5 ft (1.5 m) long.

GREAT WHITE SHARKS ARE AT THE TOP OF THE FOOD CHAIN AND ARE RARELY EATEN BY OTHER ANIMALS.

Ultimate predator

Newborn sharks feed on small fish, but as they grow to adulthood their diet expands to sea turtles, seals, dolphins, and even small whales!

You're on your own, kid

The baby sharks are completely independent once they're born. The female does not provide any motherly care and simply swims away, leaving the pups to fend for themselves.

Hungry babies

When the pups are still in the womb, they will eat their mother's unfertilized eggs! This behavior is called oophagy, and it is common in sharks. It means that once the pups are born they are as strong as possible.

GETTING UNDER MY SKIN

Suriname toad ◆ Amphibian

The female Suriname toad has a rather unusual way of caring for her babies. It starts, as most great things do, with a dance. She spins underwater with a male, who places about 100 fertilized eggs on her back using his webbed feet. Her skin then grows around the eggs! Yes, you read that right. Later, the eggs hatch inside her and the little tadpoles grow under her skin, safely protected from the outside world. We've all heard of kids getting under their parents' skin—but these toadlets take it to a whole different level!

I'm over here!

When a male wants to get a female's attention, he makes a clicking sound that can be heard underwater.

AFTER THE TOADLETS HAVE EMERGED, THE FEMALE SHEDS HER SKIN.

Time to shine

The female toad goes about her business for about three months with the baby toads in her back. When they have grown legs, the toadlets erupt through the skin on her back like zombies crawling out of the earth!

YOU'RE THE ONE THAT I WANT

Shingleback skink
♦ Reptile

Getting uncomfortable

Shingleback skinks are unusual because they don't lay eggs. Because the unborn babies are quite large, the female can't move much toward the end of her pregnancy!

Love is in the air for the female shingleback skink. Unlike most lizards she finds herself a man, and then keeps hold of him! Most reptiles will have several mates over their lifetime, but this Aussie is monogamous and will return to the same male for up to 20 years.

After the female skink becomes pregnant, she gives birth to up to four babies. The family is a tight-knit bunch, and the little skinks will stay with their parents for several months before venturing off. Even then, they don't go far!

Big baby

Shingleback babies are about 20 percent of the size of the adults when they are born.

Blue tongue

Shingleback skinks have a bright blue tongue. When threatened, they open their mouth and stick it out to make predators think they are poisonous!

Fruit bats are nocturnal, which means they are mostly active at night.

Wings of steel

Just in case you were wondering, a fruit bat baby is not small. It can be one-third of the weight of its mother! This means the moms have to be superstrong flyers.

THE BABY BATS WILL OFTEN CLING ON TO THEIR MOTHER'S NIPPLE. OUCH!

Some species of fruit bat carry their infants to a "nursery tree" where they can stay while she forages for food.

HITCH A RIDE

Fruit bat ♦ Mammal

Female fruit bats have a superpower—they can carry their pups while they fly! Baby fruit bats are born with underdeveloped wings, so they can't fly for the first few weeks of their life. During that time, the baby bats cling to the belly of their flying mother with their mouths and toes while she soars through the night sky. The caring mothers will carry and nurse their pups for several months after birth. These tandem flights are not the only time the females are required to be acrobats—they also give birth upside down!

WHO NEEDS A MAN?

While most animals need both a male and a female to create offspring, some females have a very special talent. From insects to birds, many species have found a way to reproduce without a male! These females simply clone themselves instead of worrying about finding a mate. This form of reproduction is called parthenogenesis. It is particularly useful when population numbers are low, or when it is too dangerous to mate.

Water fleas

Many species of water fleas can reproduce without the help of males. When there is plenty of food, the females will rapidly clone themselves. If food becomes scarce, the females produce "resting eggs" that are protected by a special casing. These eggs can wait several years, until more food is available, before hatching!

Ants

Some female ants can reproduce without males. *Mycocepurus smithii* is a species of ant from South America. All of the ants in each colony are clones of the queen! These clever ladies also create "fungus farms." The ants collect pieces of leaves that they feed to fungus they are growing in their nests. Once the fungus digests the plants, the ants gain even more nutrients by eating the fungus.

Stick insects

If you've ever kept a stick insect as a pet, you may have seen it lay eggs. But that's not the end of the story! If the female lays an egg that isn't fertilized by a male, that egg will hatch into a female stick insect. If the egg is fertilized by a male, it has a fifty-fifty chance of becoming a male.

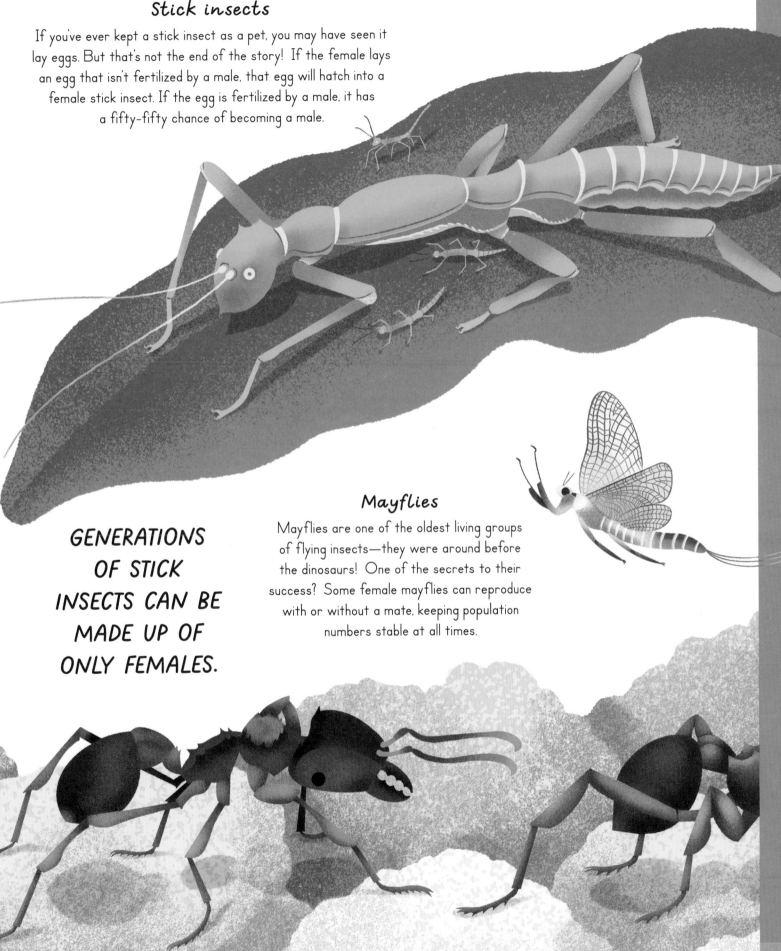

GENERATIONS OF STICK INSECTS CAN BE MADE UP OF ONLY FEMALES.

Mayflies

Mayflies are one of the oldest living groups of flying insects—they were around before the dinosaurs! One of the secrets to their success? Some female mayflies can reproduce with or without a mate, keeping population numbers stable at all times.

AMAZON WARRIORS

Amazon molly ♦ Fish

The Amazon molly is an all-female fish species—there are no males to be found! This species, named after the female Amazon warriors from Greek mythology, has survived for thousands of years by reproducing asexually. The female Amazon molly clones herself to create offspring, thereby producing only females. However, there's a twist. The females still need to perform mating behavior with a male from a closely related species to trigger the cloning process, but his genes are not passed down to the baby fish.

Clone army

Amazon mollies live in Mexico and southern USA. They have been reproducing asexually for 500,000 generations, while most asexual species go extinct at around 100,000 generations. The reason? We're not sure... Scientists are researching the Amazon molly to learn more about this exceptional species.

Tricks of the trade

After mating with a different species of molly, the Amazon molly becomes pregnant for about 45-60 days. She can also store extra sperm from the different species and use it to clone herself again very shortly after giving birth without having to mate again.

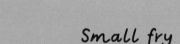

Small fry

The Amazon molly gives birth to around 60-100 baby fish called fry. The number of babies depends largely on the temperature and the amount of food available. As they're all females, it won't be long until they start cloning themselves too!

Cuddle up

Even though these females do not need to mate in order to reproduce, they are still quite affectionate with one another. Scientists think that the doting behavior witnessed between females causes a change in their hormones that makes them more likely to successfully reproduce.

LADY LIZARDS RULE

Whiptail lizard

♦ Reptile

The New Mexico whiptail lizard is another species that consists entirely of females. Unlike the Amazon molly, though, these lizards don't need any help from a male to reproduce. This is an incredible adaptation that means they do not need to spend their energy or risk being eaten by going out to find a mate. Scientists think the ability to clone themselves came as a result of the New Mexico whiptail lizard being a unique crossbreed between two different species of whiptail lizards.

Caring mother

Female California condors make their nests in cliff caves and only lay one egg at a time. They care for their offspring for more than a year, making sure they are fed, warm, and sheltered. Chicks can take as much as eight years to fully mature.

CALIFORNIA GIRLS

California condor ♦ Bird

California condors are the largest bird in North America, with a wingspan almost 10 ft (3 m) wide. They can also live for up to 60 years! Despite this, California condors almost became extinct due to habitat loss and hunting. Thankfully the feathered females of this species had a trick up their sleeve that helped to keep their population afloat. You guessed it—they can reproduce without a male!

Rewilding

In the 1980s, the California condor population was only 22 birds. Captive breeding programs, where biologists raised chicks in zoos to be released back into the wild, brought this species back from near extinction. The biologists had to get creative so the chicks didn't get used to being near humans—so they used hand puppets that looked like their parents to feed them!

The problems of parenting

Being a great mother does have its downsides. Because the female only lays one chick at a time and cares for her offspring for more than a year, California condors are slow to reproduce. Additionally, the females don't lay an egg every year, which makes them more susceptible to extinction.

ATTACK OF THE CLONES

Marbled crayfish ♦ Crustacean

So far we've seen positive examples of female-only species, but the marbled crayfish is a different story. This all-female species, if anything, is too successful! By reproducing so effectively they've become a dangerous invasive species and their populations can quickly dominate lakes and ponds. They decimate all of the plant life and snails in the area, leaving very little for the native wildlife to eat. Their habit of burrowing can also cause damage to other animals' habitats. As a result, the authorities are banning the sale of these animals!

Eggstraordinary

Each female marbled crayfish can lay up to 700 eggs in one go. These eggs develop into genetically identical offspring without the assistance of a male. This means that each female can produce thousands of clones of herself throughout her life!

Taking over

The marbled crayfish species is a result of breeding in the pet trade. This means they didn't come from anywhere in the wild. These animals were released from their aquariums and now they can be found in Europe and Asia.

MARBLED CRAYFISH CAN WALK GREAT DISTANCES TO FIND A NEW LAKE AND START A NEW POPULATION.

A LIFE OF CRIME

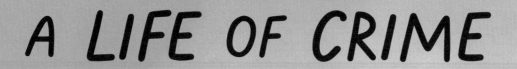

Mole salamander ♦ Amphibian

Mole salamanders are another all-female species, but unlike some of the others we've met they can't reproduce all by themselves. Although they don't need a male to produce a baby salamander, they do require male sperm to trigger the reproduction process. This leaves these ladies in a bind. What do you do when you need male sperm but you're an all-female species? The answer is to turn into thieves! Males from different salamander species leave packets of their sperm around in the same environment. The mole salamanders simply steal these packages before the females from the intended species can find them. Genius!

SALAMANDERS ARE AMPHIBIANS AND NEED WATER TO REPRODUCE.

Unsuspecting victims

The mole salamander has been known to steal sperm packets from several different species. The blue-spotted salamander, the small-mouthed salamander, and the brightly colored tiger salamander have all been victims of these master criminals.

The females transfer the packets of sperm into their reproductive tract when they are ready to reproduce.

HUNGRY
BABIES

One of the most important jobs a parent has is to keep their babies well-fed so they can grow healthy and strong. In the animal kingdom, the males of the species sometimes get involved in the feeding, but in most cases this task falls entirely on the females. Different animals feed their babies in a variety of ways to keep those tummies from rumbling.

Mother's milk

Cats, like all female mammals, produce milk to feed their offspring. This liquid is full of the nutrients babies need to grow quickly, and is their primary source of energy for the first few months of their life.

Packed lunch

Mother turtles provide a meal for their newly hatched babies through an egg yolk that stays attached to the bottom of their shell. This provides the newborns with a few days of food before they need to find their own meals.

Coming back up

Female birds feed their young with food that they have already eaten and spat back up. The babies open their mouths when they are hungry, and the mother regurgitates the digested food into their mouths—delicious!

Copy cat

Some species of spider, like jumping spiders, can produce a milklike substance to feed to their babies. This substance contains sugar, fat, and four times more protein than cow's milk!

FANCY AN ICE CREAM?

Hooded seal ♦ Mammal

Hooded seals are born in the icy world of the Arctic, but the mothers have a way of making sure their babies can withstand the unforgivable cold: they produce the fattiest milk in the animal kingdom. Up to 60 percent of their milk is fat, meaning it's as rich as ice cream! While I wouldn't recommend you eat ice cream for every meal, this diet helps the pups gain weight very quickly, in turn giving them a thick layer of fat that insulates them from the harsh cold.

Double up

By the time seal pups stop feeding on their mother's milk, they are almost twice the size they were when they were born. This is extra impressive when you consider that the pup only drinks milk for about four days!

WHEN THE PUP GROWS UP, ITS DIET CONSISTS OF FISH, SQUID, SHRIMP, STARFISH, AND EVEN OCTOPUSES.

Strict diet

When the female pigeon begins to produce crop milk she stops eating. This ensures that her milk does not get contaminated by seeds that the chicks can't digest.

Inside job

The pigeon's milk is called crop milk because it's made from a part of the bird's esophagus called the crop. This section of their body is also used for storing food.

TOP OF THE CROPS

Pigeon ♦ Bird

Like most birds, pigeons have feathers, they can fly, and they lay eggs. So far, so normal. But there's something that makes these birds a bit more unusual— they produce their own milk to feed their babies, just like mammals! Pigeon milk, called crop milk, has all of the nutrients and immune boosters that chicks need to grow strong. The female pigeon begins making this substance a few days before the eggs hatch, and she feeds the chicks for about ten days. She even gets help from the male—who can produce crop milk too!

NIBBLE AWAY

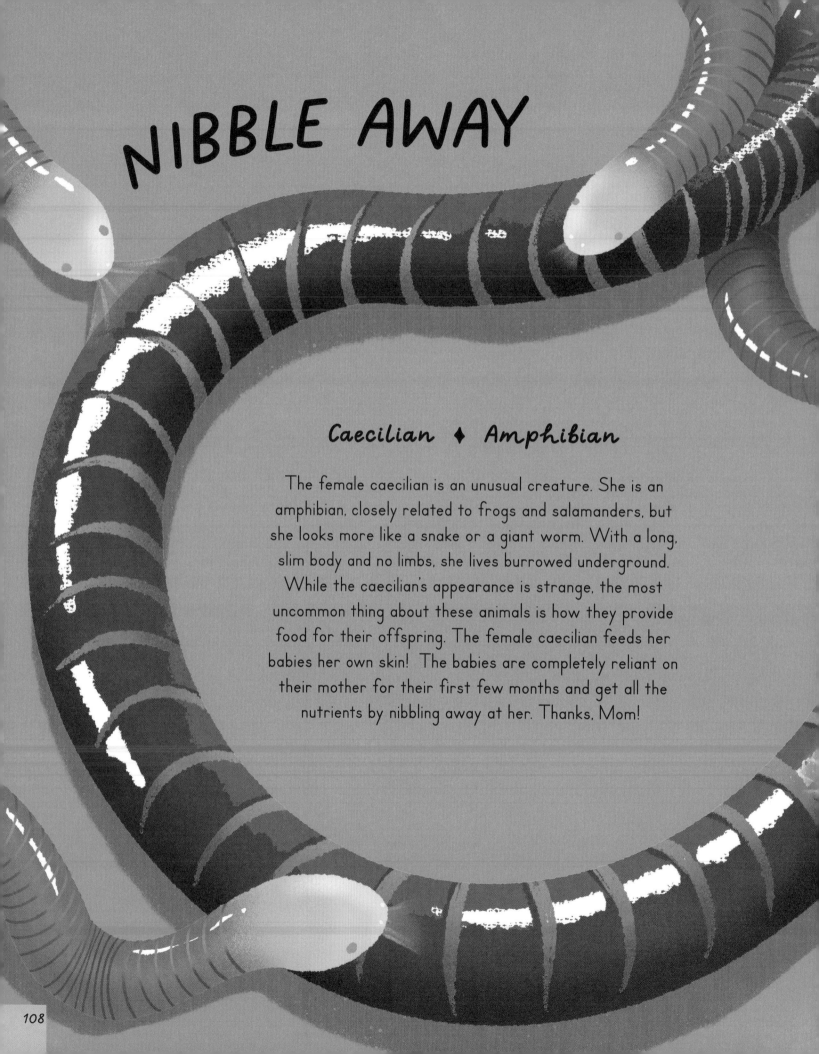

Caecilian ♦ Amphibian

The female caecilian is an unusual creature. She is an amphibian, closely related to frogs and salamanders, but she looks more like a snake or a giant worm. With a long, slim body and no limbs, she lives burrowed underground. While the caecilian's appearance is strange, the most uncommon thing about these animals is how they provide food for their offspring. The female caecilian feeds her babies her own skin! The babies are completely reliant on their mother for their first few months and get all the nutrients by nibbling away at her. Thanks, Mom!

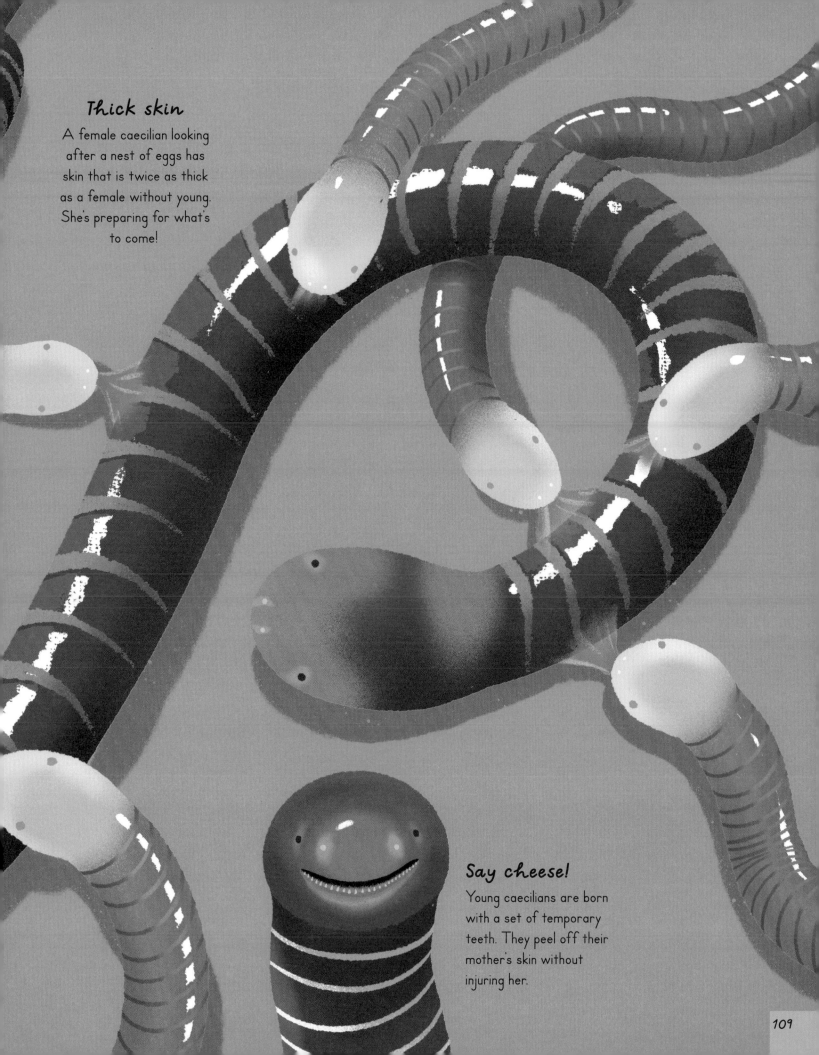

Thick skin

A female caecilian looking after a nest of eggs has skin that is twice as thick as a female without young. She's preparing for what's to come!

Say cheese!

Young caecilians are born with a set of temporary teeth. They peel off their mother's skin without injuring her.

109

WHAT'S MINE IS YOURS

Chimpanzee ♦ Primate

Moving from a milk-only diet to one that includes solid food is a big transition for many animals. Luckily, the female chimpanzee knows a trick or two to make this process easier for her young, and it's all to do with smooching... Through a method called kiss feeding, she passes food that she has already chewed in her mouth into the mouth of her offspring. This allows her to share her meals with them, especially food that is difficult to swallow or chew. Through kiss feeding, the female chimpanzee introduces her young to staple foods they will eat later in life, such as fruits, roots, and leaves. Pucker up!

Poking around

Female chimpanzees teach their young how to use tools to get a meal. One of their handy tricks is using a stick to reach inside a fire ant nest and pull out the little critters for a snack!

Precious saliva

Baby chimps swallow their mother's saliva (spit) along with the food she gives them. This helps them digest the food, which makes them grow stronger more quickly.

Vomit on the menu

The newly hatched desert spiders cluster around their mother's mouth while she throws up food (including her own digested insides!) for them to eat. The females stop repairing their sticky webs that catch prey, so the regurgitated food only comes from what she has stored in her body.

A STICKY END

Desert spider ◆ Arachnid

We've now met a few female animals that feed their babies in unusual ways, but the female desert spider takes the biscuit. Her feeding strategy is so extreme that she will only produce one clutch of eggs in her lifetime. You'll shortly see why... When they're born, desert spiders are completely helpless and need their mother to assist them as they emerge from their silk egg sac. The mother spider then feeds her offspring by regurgitating liquid food, but it's not quite enough to keep the hungry young spiders happy. So ravenous are these critters that they soon set their sights on a bigger meal. You guessed it— Mommy's on the menu! They consume every part of her that they can. The female desert spider sacrifices her own life to give her babies the best chance at life.

What's for pudding?

As the young spiders eat their mother, most of her internal organs turn into goo. Eventually all that is left of her is an exoskeleton—a hard covering that is too tough to chew.

Fluttering by

Monarch butterflies travel thousands of miles from the forests of central Mexico, where they hibernate, to meet up in the USA and Canada for the breeding season. Their descendants will make it back to Mexico.

ON THE MOVE

Many animals spend their entire lives in one place and never leave. Others undergo seasonal migrations, traveling vast distances to raise their babies somewhere with abundant food or to escape from harsh winter weather. Throughout their migrations, animals will use cues like the Earth's magnetic field to help them navigate.

The great migration

Wildebeest chase the rain across the Serengeti plains of Africa. More than a million of these animals move in an enormous loop every year in search of the lushest grasses available.

THE ARCTIC TERN HAS THE
LONGEST MIGRATION OF
ANY ANIMAL ON EARTH!

Tired wings

This water-loving bird hatches during the warmest months in the Arctic Circle. Once the cold, dark winter begins, the Arctic tern flies south, following the warm weather all the way to Antarctica, at the other end of the Earth.

The sideways march

Each year, millions of red crabs move together from their forest habitats to the beaches on their homes of Christmas Island and Cocos (Keeling) Island to breed. The female moves into a burrow dug by a male, where she'll stay to brood their eggs for about two weeks, before returning to the forest.

GIRLS' TRIP

Steelhead trout ◆ Fish

For many fish, reproducing is simple. You find a nice spot in the river and lay your eggs. Female steelhead trout, however, are anything but simple. These freshwater fish undergo epic migrations from their river homes to the middle of the Pacific Ocean. The reason? For female trout, the larger they get, the more eggs they can produce, and therefore the more babies they can have. Migrating to the ocean allows these brave ladies to eat whatever they want and reach huge sizes, before they come back to their streams when they're ready to lay eggs.

Epic adventure

Steelhead trout are native to North America and eastern Russia. The females move from inland streams to the ocean and then back to the stream to spawn, traveling for hundreds of miles. The males, however, don't need to grow to such big sizes. As a result, some of them spend their whole lives in the streams. Boring!

Are we there yet?

Through satellite tracking, scientists have discovered that loggerhead sea turtles travel all the way from beaches in Japan and Australia to the coasts of the USA, Mexico, and Peru!

Sea turtle ✦ Reptile

For female sea turtles, home is where the heart is. Every few years, they leave their foraging grounds, where they've been eating delicious sea grasses, and head back to the beach where they were born. In the dark of night, the females crawl up the familiar shoreline and dig a hole in the sand. They lay their eggs and then bury them to keep them safe. The sea turtles stay for a few weeks and lay eggs in multiple nests. Then they say a fond farewell to the beach and begin their migration back to the foraging grounds, thousands of miles away.

WHICH WAY TO THE BEACH?

Nothing to see here

The female secretly digs three to five nests and lays about 100 eggs in each. The eggs incubate under the sand for two months until the sea turtles begin to hatch. The sex of the baby turtles is determined by the temperature of the sand.

Leg it!

For the hatchlings, there's no time to check out the beach. They need to get to the ocean as fast as they can—otherwise they might end up as someone's dinner! The females that make it to adulthood will return to the same beach when they're ready to become moms.

Satellite tags are attached to the sea turtle's shell using the same stuff that is used to put fake nails on people. How fancy!

SADLY, BAY-BREASTED WARBLER POPULATIONS HAVE BEEN DECLINING OVER THE PAST FEW DECADES.

Watch out!

One of the biggest predators of warblers on their migration are birds of prey, such as hawks and owls, which will catch them in mid-air!

Bay-breasted warblers have the right idea. Instead of staying in Canada for the freezing winter, they pack their bags and head to the Caribbean for a sun-soaked getaway! Both the females and the males make this long migration, but it's one fraught with danger. Luckily the females have white and gray feathers, which makes them harder to spot. The males are far more colorful, and so less likely to make it to their vacation destination. Why are they so much more colorful if it's dangerous? It's a good question. The answer is the females prefer colorful males, so the males decided it was worth the risk!

NO NEED TO SHOW OFF

Bay-breasted warbler ♦ Bird

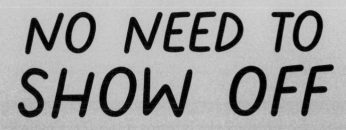

Birds of a feather

The warblers travel in flocks with birds of different species. Being in a big group helps them to keep a watch out for predators.

Vacation outfit

Scientists have discovered that there is a far bigger difference between the colors of male and female warblers that migrate than in species that stay in one place all year round. This is a result of evolution—if a female bird is more likely to survive a long journey being a more dull color, she's also more likely to reproduce.

A WHALE OF A TIME

Humpback whale

♦ Cetacean

Female humpback whales are one of the best long-distance swimmers on the planet. In fact, they have the longest migration of any mammal! During the summer, these gentle giants spend their time in cold water that's rich with their favorite foods: krill and small fish. They spend most of their time eating so they can build up fat stores to last them throughout the winter. The females then migrate up to 5,000 miles to tropical waters where they can safely raise their calves until they are ready for their long journey back to the feeding grounds.

Open wide!

Humpback whales use a technique called lunge feeding to eat vast quantities of fish. They open their mouths wide and swim upward, taking their prey by surprise from below.

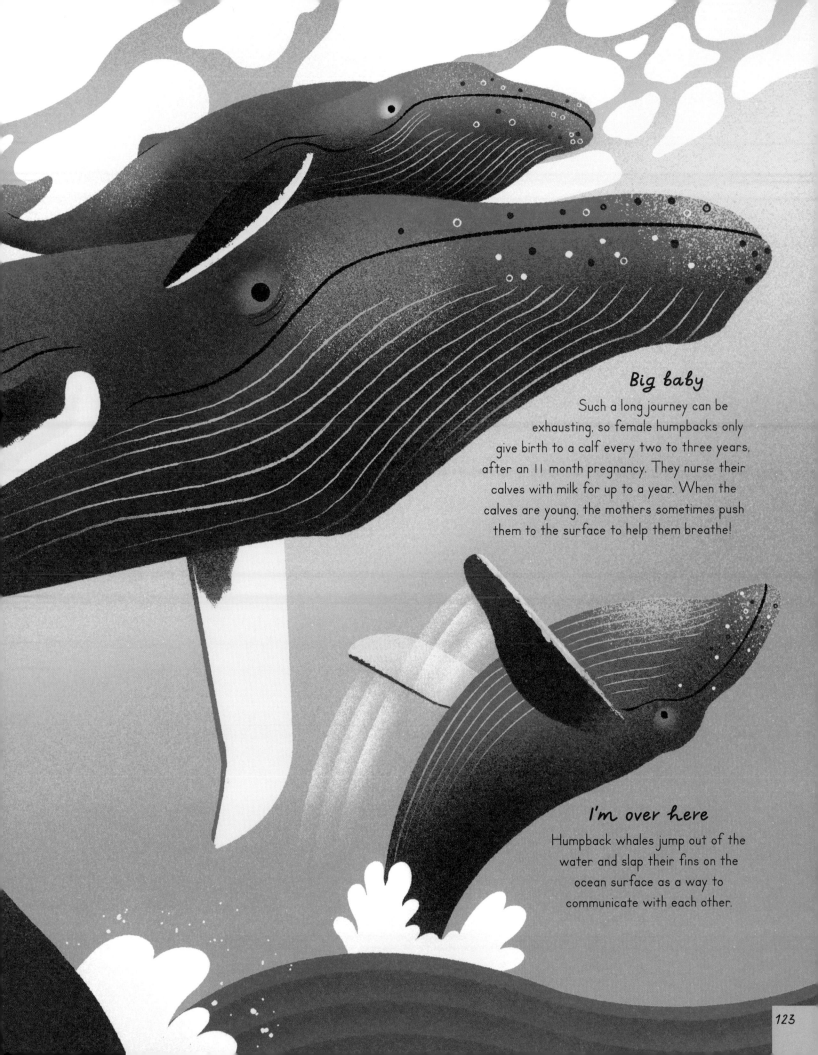

Big baby

Such a long journey can be exhausting, so female humpbacks only give birth to a calf every two to three years, after an 11 month pregnancy. They nurse their calves with milk for up to a year. When the calves are young, the mothers sometimes push them to the surface to help them breathe!

I'm over here

Humpback whales jump out of the water and slap their fins on the ocean surface as a way to communicate with each other.

GLOSSARY

Amphibian A type of animal that can live both on land and in water. Frogs, toads, and salamanders are examples of amphibians.

Arachnid A type of animal with eight legs. Spiders and scorpions are examples of arachnids.

Biologist A scientist who studies living things, like animals and plants.

Brood A group of babies that an animal cares for at the same time.

Burrow A hole or tunnel in the ground that an animal lives in.

Carnivore An animal that eats meat.

Cephalopod A soft-bodied animal that lives underwater and has arms and sometimes tentacles. Examples of cephalopods are octopuses, squid, and cuttlefish.

Cetacean A type of large sea animal that breathes air. Whales and dolphins are examples of cetaceans.

Chromosome Part of a cell inside an animal that carries genes. Genes act as instructions for how the animal looks and functions.

Clone An exact copy of another living thing.

Cocoon A protective covering that some insects make around themselves before they change into their adult form. For example, caterpillars create a cocoon before they transform into butterflies.

Colony A group of the same kind of animals living together.

Feeding frenzy When a lot of animals eat at the same time.

Genes Instructions in our cells that help decide things like our hair color, eye color, and height.

Habitat The natural environment where an animal or plant lives.

Herbivore An animal that eats only plants.

Hibernation A state of deep sleep some animals go into, usually during winter, to save energy.

Hierarchy A system that ranks members of a group from least important to most important.

Mammal A type of animal that feeds their babies with milk. Humans, cats, and whales are examples of mammals.

Marsupial A type of mammal that carries its babies in a pouch. Kangaroos and koalas are examples of marsupials.

Matriarch The female leader of a group.

Migration The act of animals traveling to a different place, often because of the changing seasons, to find food, or to go to somewhere safe to have their babies (sometimes all of the above).

Monotreme A type of mammal that lays eggs. Platypuses and echidnas are monotremes.

Nectar A sweet liquid inside flowers that attracts animals, who in turn will help the flowers to reproduce.

Neurotoxin A type of poison that can harm the brain and nervous system.

Offspring The babies of an animal.

Omnivore An animal that eats both plants and meat.

Parasite A living thing that lives on or in another organism (its host) and benefits at the expense of its host.

Predator An animal that hunts and eats other animals.

Prey An animal that gets hunted and eaten by other animals.

Primate A type of furry mammal with a big brain and opposable thumbs. Examples of primates include lemurs, monkeys, and humans.

Scavenger An animal that eats dead animals that it finds (and didn't hunt itself).

Shedding When animals lose their old fur or skin to make way for new growth.

Tundra A cold, treeless area, often found in Antarctica or the Arctic. A tundra is a type of desert.

Venom A toxic substance that some animals produce to protect themselves or to catch their food.

INDEX

This has been a

NEON SQUID
production

This book is dedicated to the future female leaders of our world. I hope you will be inspired by the strength of the lionesses, wisdom of the elephants, power of the trap-jaw ants, and the industriousness of the bees. We eagerly await the brilliance of your future contributions.

Author: Dr. Carly Anne York
Illustrator: Kimberlie Clinthorne-Wong
Consultant: Dr. Brittney G. Borowiec

Editorial Assistant: Malu Rocha
US Editor: Jill Freshney
Proofreader: Joseph Barnes
Indexer: Elizabeth Wise

Printed and bound in Guangdong, China by Leo Paper Products Ltd.

ISBN: 978-1-684-49374-6

Published in May 2024.

www.neonsquidbooks.com

About the author

Dr Carly Anne York is a scientist and author who studies how animals interact with their environments. She is also a biology professor and science communicator who has collaborated with TED-Ed on the creation of science lessons, participated in YouTube shows and podcasts, and been featured on the Science Channel. Carly also runs an animal sanctuary and owns several horses!

About the illustrator

Kimberlie Clinthorne-Wong is an illustrator, designer, and ceramicist from Hawaii. She travels between tropical Honolulu and temperate Michigan with her family. Kimberlie's diverse range of work includes conceptual editorials to whimsically surreal and playfully imagined worlds for children's illustrations.